Con...

**Jan Burchett
and Sara Vogler**

**Story illustrated by
Tom Percival**

Heinemann

Find out about

- Stonehenge – the ancient circle of huge stones

Tricky words

- archaeologists
- enormous
- weighed
- machines
- worshipped
- magician
- soldiers
- figures

Introduce these tricky words and help the reader when they come across them later!

Text starter

Stonehenge is a circle of huge stones built over 5000 years ago. Today, many of the stones have fallen down. Archaeologists have tried to find out how the huge stones got to Stonehenge. There are also many legends explaining how the stones got there.

Building Stonehenge

What is Stonehenge?

Stonehenge is a circle of huge stones.
It was built over 5000 years ago.
Some of the stones have fallen down
but many of them are still standing today.
Archaeologists have tried to find out how
the huge stones got to Stonehenge.

How did people move the stones?

Stonehenge was made of 82 enormous stones. Some of the stones weighed more than five large elephants!

So how did people in the past who had no machines and no roads move such enormous stones?

Archaeologists think that each stone needed 500 men to drag it along! The men put down rollers in front of the stones. The rollers were made from tree trunks. Then the men pulled the stones over the rollers using long ropes. It was hard work!

When the stone was at the front of the rollers, the men took the rollers from the back to the front so that they could pull the stone forward again.

Where did the stones come from?

Some of the stones at Stonehenge came from 250 miles away in South Wales. Sometimes the stones were taken on a raft along the river. But most of the time they were dragged over the ground. The men had to get the stones up and down lots of hills.

In summer people go to Stonehenge to see the sun rise.

Sun worship

Archaeologists think people worshipped the sun at Stonehenge thousands of years ago. There is a stone altar in the middle of the circle. In the middle of the summer, the first rays of the sun at dawn hit the stone altar.

The face on the stone

When the sun's rays hit one of the stones some people say that you can see a face on the stone. They say that this is the face of Merlin, who was the magician in the stories of King Arthur.

Legends about Stonehenge

In one legend it says that 300 of King Arthur's soldiers were killed in a terrible battle. King Arthur was very sad about all the soldiers who had died. He wanted everyone to remember them so he asked Merlin what he should do.

Merlin told King Arthur to build a circle of stones that would last for ever. But there were no big stones nearby, so Merlin used his magical powers to make some huge stones fly all the way from Ireland. And that is why there is a circle of stones at Stonehenge today.

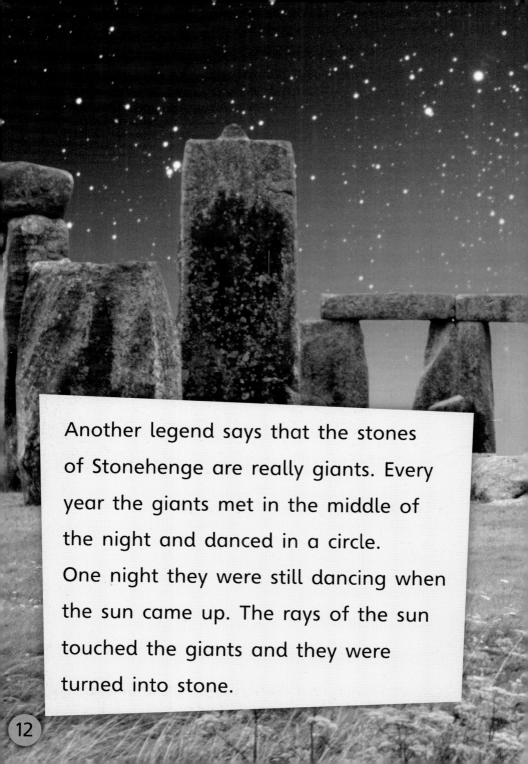

Another legend says that the stones
of Stonehenge are really giants. Every
year the giants met in the middle of
the night and danced in a circle.
One night they were still dancing when
the sun came up. The rays of the sun
touched the giants and they were
turned into stone.

The legend says that the wind and the rain have worn away all the figures of the giants, but sometimes when the rays of the sun touch the stones, the faces of the giants appear.

Another legend says that the name Stonehenge means 'hanging stone' because about 3000 years ago Stonehenge was the place where criminals were hanged, and that is how it got its name.

There are many different legends about Stonehenge but could any of them be true?

Quiz

Text Detective

- How were the stones moved?
- What facts can you remember about Stonehenge?

Word Detective

- **Phonic Focus:** Vowel phonemes in polysyllabic words

  Page 4: How many syllables are there in 'elephants'? What vowel phoneme can you hear in each syllable?
- Page 4: Find two adjectives.
- Page 6: Find a word meaning 'drag'.

Super Speller

Read these words:

many enormous middle

Now try to spell them!

HA! HA! HA!

Q What does a magician have up his sleeve?

A His arm!

15

Before Reading

In this story

 Carla

 Rob

 Dad

Introduce these tricky words and help the reader when they come across them later!

Tricky words

- circle
- eclipse
- worshipping
- sacrificed
- magician
- haunts
- image
- staring

Story starter

Carla's and Rob's dad is an archaeologist. He finds out about people who lived long ago. One summer, Carla and Rob went with their dad to the ancient stone circle of Stonehenge. He wanted to find out about the people who built Stonehenge.

The Face on the Stone

Carla and Rob helped Dad to set up their camp near Stonehenge.

"This stone circle is very old," said Dad. "It was built about 5000 years ago. The team are going to dig near here. We want to find out about the people who built Stonehenge."

"Oh! I nearly forgot," said Dad. "There is going to be an eclipse of the sun today."

"What is an eclipse?" asked Rob.

"It's when the moon passes in front of the sun," said Dad. "For a few minutes it will get as dark as night!"

"Why was Stonehenge built?" asked Carla.

"Nobody knows!" said Dad. "Some people think it was a place for worshipping the sun, or a place where people were sacrificed."

"Spooky!" said Rob. "I want to find out more about Stonehenge."

Rob went to the shop and got a book. "Hey!" he said to Carla. "You remember Merlin the magician in the King Arthur stories? Well, it says here that Merlin used magic to bring the stones from Ireland. They flew through the air."

"Rubbish!" said Carla. "That's impossible!"

"Listen to this," said Rob as he read on. "There is a legend that says that Merlin still haunts Stonehenge. He appears when there is an eclipse."

"That's rubbish too," said Carla. "Merlin wasn't a real person. He's only in stories and films."

It was getting dark. The eclipse was beginning. Dad said that it was dangerous to look straight at the sun and they would need to use mirrors to reflect the sun's image on to one of the stones.

Rob decided to play a trick on Carla.
"I'm going to watch the eclipse from
over there," he said, and he went off.

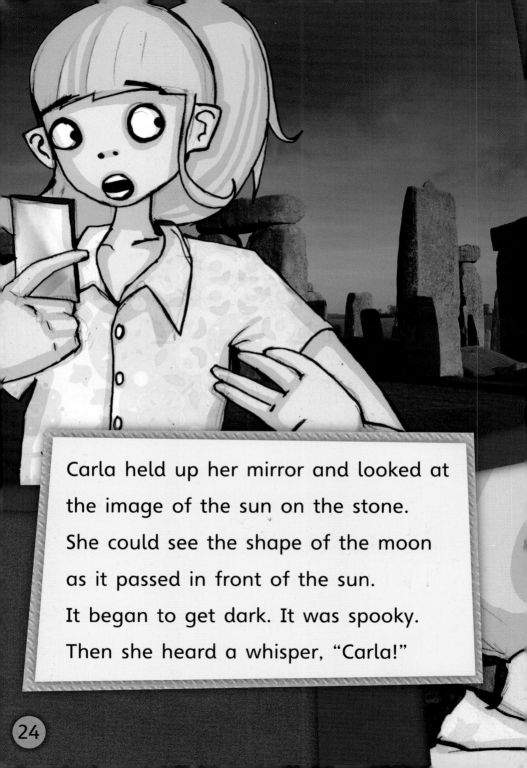

Carla held up her mirror and looked at the image of the sun on the stone. She could see the shape of the moon as it passed in front of the sun. It began to get dark. It was spooky. Then she heard a whisper, "Carla!"

She spun round. She could see somebody in the dim light. He was wearing a long robe and a pointed hat. Was it Merlin? Carla was scared. Then she saw a trainer sticking out from the robe. It wasn't Merlin after all. It was Rob!

"I know it's you, Rob!" she shouted.

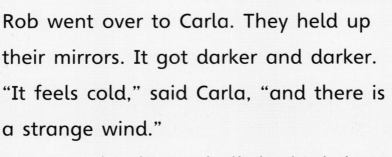

Rob went over to Carla. They held up their mirrors. It got darker and darker.

"It feels cold," said Carla, "and there is a strange wind."

"Yes," said Rob, "and all the birds have stopped singing. It's really spooky."

A total solar eclipse occurs every 365 years!

As the moon went in front of the sun it got very dark. The edges of the moon were glowing.

"It's beautiful," said Carla.

Then it began to get lighter.

Rob pointed at one of the stones.

"Cool!" he said. "How did you do that trick, Carla?"

"What trick?" asked Carla.

"Can't you see the face on the stone?" asked Rob. He sounded scared.

Carla looked at the stone.

Rob was right – there *was* a face on it.
It was as big as the stone and it was
staring straight at them.

"It's not a trick," whispered Carla. "I didn't
do that."

As it got lighter, the face disappeared. Carla and Rob ran towards the stone. They looked carefully at it. There were lots of bumps on the stone but no staring face.

"Do you think it was the strange light that made the face appear?" asked Rob. "I don't know," said Carla. "It could have been the light shining on the bumps on the stone. Or maybe the stories are true and it *was* Merlin!"

Quiz

Text Detective

- Why did Carla use a mirror to look at the sun?
- Do you think Rob played a good trick on Carla?

Word Detective

- **Phonic Focus:** Vowel phonemes in polysyllabic words
  Page 17: Sound out the four phonemes in 'people'. Which letters make the long 'ee' phoneme?
- Page 25: Find a word made up of two shorter words.
- Page 26: Find words ending in 'er'.

Super Speller

Read these words:

people somebody nobody

Now try to spell them!

HA! HA! HA!

Q What do a footballer and a magician have in common?

 They both do hat tricks!

32